Moving On

Three Short Plays

by Maureen Brady Johnson

Baker's Plays
7611 Sunset Blvd.
Los Angeles, CA 90042
bakersplays.com

NOTICE

This book is offered for sale at the price quoted only on the understanding that, if any additional copies of the whole or any part are necessary for its production, such additional copies will be purchased. The attention of all purchasers is directed to the following: this work is fully protected under the copyright laws of the United States of America, the British Commonwealth, including Canada, and all other countries of the Copyright Union. Violations of the Copyright Law are punishable by fine or imprisonment, or both. The copying or duplication of this work or any part of this work, by hand or by any process, is an infringement of the copyright and will be vigorously prosecuted.

This play may not be produced by amateurs or professionals for public or private performance without first submitting application for performing rights. Royalties are due on all performances whether for charity or gain, or whether admission is charged or not Since performance of this play without the payment of the royalty fee renders anybody participating liable to severe penalties imposed by the law, anybody acting in this play should be sure, before doing so, that the royalty fee has been paid. Professional rights, reading rights, radio broadcasting, television and all mechanical rights, etc. are strictly reserved. Application for performing rights should be made directly to BAKER'S PLAYS.

No one shall commit or authorize any act or omission by which the copyright of, or the right to copyright, this play may be impaired. No one shall make any changes in this play for the purpose of production.

Publication of this play does not imply availability for performance. Both amateurs and professionals considering a production are strongly advised in their own interest to apply to Baker's Plays for written permission before starting rehearsals, advertising, or booking a theatre.

Whenever the play is produced, the author's name must be carried in all publicity, advertising and programs. Also, the following notice must appear on all printed programs, "Produced by special arrangement with Baker's Plays."

Licensing fees for *MOVING ON* is based on a per performance rate and payable one week in advance of the production.

Please consult the Baker's Plays website at www.bakersplays.com or our current print catalogue for up to date licensing fee information.

CONTENTS

ROCK PAPER SCISSORS

Synopsis

Socrates said, "Know thyself." Kate, Butterfly and Dottie are roommates who think they do. But when they try to explain what happens one crazy afternoon, they declare that there is no fault in not knowing yourself at all. Socrates may disagree.

Setting

Three lit areas onstage

Characters

BUTTERFLY - 27. She is a hippie-wannabe. Occupies the first area.

KATE - 27. A new mother who'd rather be doing anything else. Occupies the second area.

DOTTIE - 27. Definitely a pastel green person who swears there is a neon yellow inside her dying to get out. Occupies the third area.

Costumes

BUTTERFLY - Hippie clothes from the 70s.

KATE - Jeans, t-shirt, perhaps a bit too tight.

DOTTIE - Jeans and a t-shirt spattered with neon yellow paint.

Props

BUTTERFLY - her beads.

KATE - her baby (doll).

DOTTIE - her paint, in a can or on a paint brush.

Each actress should freeze in a pose after her piece is said. They do not hear each other speak.

ROCK, PAPER, SCISSORS was a 2001 finalist and nominated for the Heidemann Award in the ATL National Ten-Minute Play Contest.

ROCK, PAPER, SCISSORS was first produced by:

The Brief Acts Company
A Division of Love Creek Productions Network
The Parker Theatre at the Algonquin Theatre
123 East 24th St. New York City
July 23, 24 and 25, 2008

Directed by Steven Barrett
Cast: Melanie DeBernadis, Rebecca Rose McCain and Jessica Bishop

BUTTERFLY. It all started with Kate breastfeeding that brat on the bus. She should have known better. Maybe she should have let the kid scream. But, no. She just went ahead and whipped out that boob and that's when the trouble started. *(freeze)*

KATE. Those stupid beads. Butterfly never should have taken them on the bus. That's when the trouble started. She insisted on taking all of them. Then, she started threading them on the bus. Those stupid, stupid beads. *(freeze)*

DOTTIE. Actually, it was my fault. I think it was my idea to paint the statue in the square. Should be neon...neon yellow. I love neon yellow. *(pause)* I think it was my fault. *(freeze)*

BUTTERFLY. The kid has a scream that kills flying insects within a 10 mile radius. I know that Kate had to bring the baby, being the only source of nutrition and all. AND, I'm as liberal as the next when it comes to breastfeeding in public. But when the weather turned hot and sweaty, she should have known the kid wasn't going to sleep for long. Maybe it was the baby's fault. *(freeze)*

KATE. I told her, "Butterfly, do not take every last bead you own. We are only going crosstown. How many beads do you think you can string in 45 minutes?"
She should have thought about the buss lurching and jerking and put the beads into something more secure. I never thought it would lead to this. *(freeze)*

DOTTIE. I AM a neon yellow person, no matter what my friends say. Y'know, there's a book I read that divides the whole human race into colors. You got your dreamers, purple...your type-A reds...your losers, greasy gray. I read the whole book, took the test and the closest I came to being a color was a pastel green. Not emerald green or forest green or even chartreuse. Pukey pastel green. So, I figured I needed to make a statement, for all those that sit on the back of the bus or in the last desk of the last row of the classroom, beaten down by society and labeled by a stupid book as pastel green when they know that there is a neon yellow inside them, dying to get out. *(freeze)*

BUTTERFLY. I could actually see people developing major twitches right before my eyes. Oh yeah, they started out with the, "Oh, I got a fruit fly on my eyebrow"-type twitches. But as the kid revved up, turning that shade of reddish purple that the kid always turns, I saw twitches on parts of the human body that were never meant to twitch. *(freeze)*

KATE. Butterfly thinks that she can make a living stringing those beads. Problem is that she won't part with them. She strings them, calling each one by name.

"Here you go little 'Greeny'. Free from the box and out in the world. Aren't you pretty? Next is 'Bluey', your little friend."

She gets so attached to them that she hasn't sold a necklace yet. She just likes setting the beads free. *(freeze)*

DOTTIE. What could I paint that would make a statement? A coming out statement. *(pause)*

Of course. My closet!

But the landlord would get mad if I painted the outside of the closet and end up keeping our security deposit. So I decided to paint the **inside** of the closet neon yellow. I told Kate and Butterfly that I was going out. I said, "I need to get some plain yogurt", just to mislead them. They think I'm a pastel green. *(freeze)*

BUTTERFLY. Why does that kid scream so much? She screams when Kate comes in at 2 am. She screams whenever some of the guys come over to drink and when we crank up the music to dance in the hallway. It's not normal.

As she screamed, she oozed.

Baby spit dribbled onto Kate's shoulders giving her those little epaulets of puke that parents have. I tried to protect my beads. *(freeze)*

KATE. I held the baby so she wouldn't drool on the beads. Butterfly is real particular about who or what touches her beads. Once, the baby disappeared for about an hour and I found her under the bed in Butterfly's room eating one of her mother-of-pearls. *(freeze)*

DOTTIE. I'd never been in a shop like this before. There were always a lot of very weird people in there. But it was the only place in town that sold buckets of neon paint. The college kids use it to paint their rooms. I took a deep breath, opened the door and was hit with a cloud of *(pause)* patchouli. *(freeze)*

BUTTERFLY. I considered shoving a couple of beads up my nose to stop the smell. But I couldn't figure out which beads to sacrifice.
The kid screamed. Everyone on the bus was thinking of doing something drastic, twitching the whole time. Who could have known what was going to happen next? *(freeze)*

KATE. I had no choice. Everyone on the bus was turning against me.
"What kind of a mother is she? Can't she keep that baby quiet?" I had to do something. *(freeze)*

DOTTIE. I had a vision. *(freeze)*

BUTTERFLY. I never thought she'd whip out her boob in public. I dropped my beads. Everything went into slow motion after that. The boob, the kid, my beads dropping, one by one on the floor. It was like those running dreams where something is chasing you and your feet are too heavy. Slow motion and surreal. *(freeze)*

KATE. Good mothers breastfeed. *(freeze)*

DOTTIE. The statue. Paint the statue in the square. I bought the paint and took off through the park, trying to look nonchalant. I mean after all, my pastel life was about to go Neon. I hid behind a bush and I stirred the paint. The brush shook in my hand. I couldn't paint with the shakes. What would Butterfly do right now? She'd say, "Screw the brush. Throw the paint." *(freeze)*

BUTTERFLY. So there I am getting my designer bell bottoms filthy, crawling around on my knees, trying to pick up the beads.
"Excuse me. Sorry.
Could you please lift your foot." *(freeze)*

KATE. Have you ever had an entire bus turn against you? *(freeze)*

DOTTIE. I took the can, jumped out from behind the bush, closed my eyes, screamed something like, "The hell with my closet." and threw the paint. *(freeze)*

BUTTERFLY. It wasn't my fault that the beads rolled under the foot of the bus driver. *(freeze)*

KATE. So the bus starts weaving all over the road – jumps the curb and heads for the statue on the square. But I kept feeding the kid. No one is going to call me a bad mother, least of all a bunch of losers on the bus. *(freeze)*

DOTTIE. I look up and the bus is coming right at me. I tried to get out of the way, slipped on the neon yellow, and hit my head on a rock. As I passed out, I heard a baby crying. *(freeze)*

BUTTERFLY. What was I supposed to do? People were stepping on my precious beads. *(freeze)*

KATE. When the bus hit the statue, my boob popped out of the baby's mouth. And she started crying again. *(freeze)*

DOTTIE. Yes, I heard a baby crying. *(freeze)*

BUTTERFLY. I got all the beads, but the baby started crying, again. I think it was after the bus hit the statue. *(freeze)*

KATE. Those stupid beads. It wasn't my fault she dropped the beads. *(freeze)*

DOTTIE. The statue stopped the bus. *(pleased)* When I came to, I was covered in neon yellow.

*(**BUTTERFLY** and **KATE** say the following line simultaneously. **DOTTIE** says her line just a hair slower than the other two.)*

BUTTERFLY.	**KATE.**
It wasn't my fault.	It wasn't my fault.

    DOTTIE. It probably was my fault.

BUTTERFLY. I was just setting them free. *(freeze)*

KATE. I AM a good mother. *(freeze)*

DOTTIE. I am NOT pastel green. *(freeze)*

(blackout)

OFFSTAGE VOICE. Guilty.

The End

HARVESTING THE MARIGOLD SEEDS

Synopsis

This play is about balance. It is about knowing when to change and move on with your life while preserving those things that connect us to the past.

Mary shows up at an exercise emporium called "Shake It Out" to work out with her friends, Camille, Annie and Grace. Mary's mom has already called three times from the graduated care facility where she now lives to remind her to collect the marigold seeds from her garden. Mary, who has lived with her mom her entire life, decides that for the first time in her life, she has the freedom to plant the kind of flowers in her yard she has always wanted to grow. Camille and Grace are horrified at the prospect of losing the prize-winning marigold seeds. Annie thinks that Mary should be able to plant whatever she wants to. Urged on by the tape recorded voice at "Shake It Out," Mary has to decide whether she will collect the heirloom seeds or 'Move on' with her life.

I wrote this play after a year of exercising at "Curves." The friends I have made while exercising have shared the most incredible stories with me while we are flailing our arms and legs about. The tape recorded voice, 'Move on, please' serves as a metaphor for our lives.

As a child, my mother would collect the marigold seeds for the next spring when they were planted. I have fond memories of collecting the seeds with her. I still harvest the marigold seeds with my own daughters. It is a tradition worth saving, passed down from generation to generation.

Characters

MARY - 48, single. Teacher. Lived at home all of her life taking care of her mother who just recently entered an assisted living home. Wears a big-eyed cat t-shirt to exercise.

CAMILLE - Late 50s, married. Gently opinionated. She wears a t-shirt to exercise that says, "Good Morning is an oxymoron".

ANNIE - 28. Teaches dance at the local college. Wears a "Race for the Cure" t-shirt.

GRACE - Late 60s to 70s. Potter/Gallery owner. Wears a t-shirt that says "Art. Ask for More".

All the actresses "exercise" throughout the play. The cast should pace themselves.

11

VOICE - An offstage voice at the exercise place. This voice tells the women when to change stations and when to check their pulses.

THE VOICE OF MARY'S MOM - An offstage or recorded voice or a small walk-on.

Props

None are necessary but water bottles, towels, etc. can be used.

The Setting

The simple set represents an exercise place. Three slightly raised platforms with three chairs in between each platform on the stage. These represent six exercise stations.

The time is 7 am and the day is Saturday.

HARVESTING THE MARIGOLD SEEDS was first performed at the Red Hen Theatre Cleveland, Ohio for three weekends in June, 2005. It was directed by Rose Leininger.
Original cast members: Kate Duffield (Camille), Annie Little (Grace), Kristi Little (Annie), and Christine Winsberg (Mary). Kathy Sullivan was the voice.

HARVESTING THE MARIGOLD SEEDS was a second place winner for the Little Theatre of Alexandria's One Act Play contest.

HARVESTING THE MARIGOLD SEEDS won the 2008 Kansas City Women's Playwriting Contest and Festival and was performed at the Potluck Theatre March 7 through March 16.

*(**AT RISE:** Stage is dark. Audience hears a phone ringing 3 times. Answering machine picks up.)*

MARY'S VOICE. Hi. Thanks for calling. The only one home is the cat. I'm probably exercising. Leave a detailed message and I will call you within the next 24 hours. Or you could call my cell.

VOICE OF MARY'S MOM. It's 5:30. I can't believe you're not up yet. Mary, today is the perfect day to harvest the marigold seeds. You're on your own now. I can't help you with this anymore. Call me when you get this message.

(She hangs up. Pause.)

(Phone rings 3 times. Answering machine picks up.)

MARY'S VOICE. Hi. Thanks for calling. The only one home is the cat. I'm probably exercising. Leave a detailed message and I will call you within the next 24 hours. Or you could call my cell.

VOICE OF MARY'S MOM. It's 6. Aren't you awake yet? Make sure you keep the marigold seeds separate. Don't mix up the varieties. The America Beautiful committee can tell the difference between a Queen Sophia and a Flagstaff. That contest has been won the past five years on the heirloom quality of my marigolds and if you get them all mixed up I don't know what will happen.

Just because I don't live there any more doesn't mean you can get sloppy. And don't share those seeds with anyone, especially Camille. She's wanted to get her hands on them for years. Those marigold seeds stay in our family. Some of those seeds belonged to my great grandmother.

(She hangs up. Pause.)

(Phone rings 3 times. Answering machine picks up.)

MARY'S VOICE. Hi. Thanks for calling. The only one home is the cat. I'm probably exercising. Leave a detailed message and I will call you within the next 24 hours. Or you could call my cell.

VOICE OF MARY'S MOTHER. Mary. I know you are there. Pick up the phone.

(She sighs.)

I've been calling every half hour to catch you before you go to exercise. No one around here is up yet. I'm just sitting here remembering the early morning coffee we used to have together. Your coffee is so much better than what they have here. You knew how to make a good, strong cup not like the colored water they serve here. I really miss it.

Mary, don't forget to collect the marigold seeds from around the pond. The black snake won't hurt you. Oh, and Mary, if you see Annie at exercise tell her I am very sorry I didn't get to her dance concert.

(She hangs up. Pause.)

(Phone rings 3 times. Answering machine picks up.)

MARY'S VOICE. Hi. Thanks for calling. The only one home is the cat. I'm probably exercising. Leave a detailed message and I will call you within the next 24 hours. Or you could call my cell.

VOICE OF MARY'S MOM. It's 7 o'clock. You must be exercising. I forgot to tell you where to put the marigold seeds after you harvest them. There are blue canning jars in the shed. They all have chipped lids so the seeds will dry properly. Call me when you get in. And Mary, why don't I have your cell phone number?

(Lights come up. Upbeat music plays. CAMILLE enters and begins to exercise at the first station stage right. When the actresses change stations they move from stage right to stage left.)

VOICE. Move on please.

(MARY enters right and begins to exercise at station one. CAMILLE enters and begins to exercise. Music should fade but still play softly in the background.)

CAMILLE. Hey, Mary.

MARY. Hey, Camille.

CAMILLE. Happy Saturday morning. You're up kind of early.

MARY. Mom called at 5:30 this morning and wants me to collect the marigold seeds from the yard today.

CAMILLE. At five thirty in the morning?

MARY. And then she called at 6 and at 6:30.

CAMILLE. What did she want at 6?

MARY. She wanted to make sure I kept the seeds to each kind of marigold separate. And to keep every last one of them. I am not allowed to share her heirloom seeds with anyone.

CAMILLE. And at 6:30?

MARY. She didn't want me to forget the marigolds around the pond in the back. She knows I don't like to go back by the pond because I saw a big black snake back there when I was 12.

CAMILLE. Why is she so worried about her marigold seeds?

MARY. I don't know. She knows that it's my job to harvest the seeds each year. Every fall since I was six she had a list of things she wanted me to do around her yard. Rake the leaves. Plant the garlic. Pinch the mums. Collect the marigold seeds. Honestly. You'd think she'd know that I don't need to be reminded every year to do this stuff.

CAMILLE. She misses doing it herself. She loved to putter around in that garden of hers.

MARY. I wouldn't call it puttering…I'd call it obsessing. And she's so afraid that I will forget to do something. I'm almost 50 years old. I think I can remember to collect the marigold seeds. She still treats me like a child.

CAMILLE. When you're a mom, your kids never grow up. My daughter's here from Florida. She's 32, a personal trainer, runnin' her own business, been livin' on her own for years and the minute she walked in my house she says, "Momma, can you cook your chili and cornbread for me?" I said, "Got some waitin' for you." The minute she walked in the door and asked for my chili and cornbread, she turned into my little girl and I turned into her momma.

MARY. I know. But I've been taking care of her yard all my life. I have never forgotten to collect those seeds. I just wish she'd give me some credit.

CAMILLE. Her marigolds looked so good this year. Where did she ever get the idea to plant them in that old tree stump?

MARY. Actually, that was my idea. When the cherry tree blew down in that storm last year I just couldn't bear to get rid of the stump that was left. I loved that tree. I used to climb in it when I was a kid and eat cherries until I was sick. So I filled it up with dirt and made it into a planter. Mom thought it looked too messy for the yard. A big old stump smack-dab in the middle of the lawn. "Nothing will grow in that old stump" and she fussed at me until a neighbor walked by when she was working in the yard and said, "I love those marigolds growing in that old stump." And they stood there oohing and ahhing about it for a good fifteen minutes. She never bothered me about it again.

VOICE. Move on please.

(**MARY** and **CAMILLE** move to the next station. **ANNIE** enters and begins at station one.)

ANNIE. Mornin'.

CAMILLE & MARY. Mornin' Annie.

MARY. I wonder what would happen if I didn't collect the marigold seeds this year?

ANNIE. What's this about collecting marigold seeds?

CAMILLE. Mary's mom called at 5:30 this morning to remind her to collect the marigold seeds.

ANNIE. Why not just buy new plants? I buy new plants every year.

CAMILLE. You don't know Mary's mother, do you, Annie?

ANNIE. Not really. I've seen her working in her yard and stopped to talk. She comes to all my dance concerts at the college. Why?

CAMILLE. I've known that woman for years and she is very particular. And if there's one thing she is extremely per-snickety about, it's her marigolds. She will not share those seeds with anyone. How old are those seeds now, Mary?

MARY. I think they qualify for heirloom status. But they are a pain to collect. There are so many of them. Front yard, back yard, side yard, by the fountain, around the edges of the shed and way out by the pond. It takes forever. I may just skip it this year. I mean, it's really my yard now that she's not living at home.

ANNIE. Why does she plant so many of them?

MARY. They keep pests out of the garden. Bugs don't like them.

ANNIE. Well, they are the prettiest bug control I've ever seen. Your yard always looks nice. I can't keep up with mine.

MARY. I know. I'm beginning to feel the same way. Now that Mom isn't there to take care of it with me, it's overwhelming. I have other things to do besides collect her prize marigold seeds.

VOICE. Move on please.

(**MARY, CAMILLE, ANNIE** *change stations and* **GRACE** *enters.*)

GRACE. Good morning everybody.

ALL. Mornin' Grace.

GRACE. What's the scuttlebutt this morning?

CAMILLE. Mary doesn't want to harvest the marigold seeds.

GRACE. Does your mother know about this?

MARY. Not yet.

GRACE. I don't want to be around when you tell her.

MARY. I'm not going to tell her. It's time I made some changes. To tell you the truth, I never liked the smell of those marigolds. Maybe I'll plant nasturtiums next year. I've always liked them. Did you know you can eat them?

CAMILLE. If you plant nasturtiums, I do believe that the world will come to an end.

GRACE. Camille is right, Mary. Those are prize winning marigolds. They win blue ribbons at the county fair every year. You can't NOT collect the seeds.

CAMILLE. Your mother's yard is one of the cornerstones of our city. Remember five years ago when that "Beautiful America" committee came to this town for the first time? They walked around this city with those polite smiles on their faces looking at this and that. I think they expected just another small town trying real hard to measure up to the big town competition. Why, when they got to your mother's house, those smiles fell right off their faces. They were truly impressed. They couldn't believe those marigolds...All the different types and colors. I swear those marigolds won that contest for us single handedly and we've won every year since. Those judges go directly to your mother's house now just to see her marigolds. You just can't let this city down. You've got to collect those seeds and plant them next year.

(MARY stops exercising.)

MARY. Look, I have spent too much of my life collecting those seeds and if I want to live it up a little and plant nasturtiums or gladiolas or even those smelly, exotic castor bean plants...I WILL.

VOICE. Stop. Time to check your heart rate. Ready. Begin.

(The women stop exercising and check their pulse. Some check their wrist pulse, some check their neck pulse. No one talks. The music continues to play in the background.)

VOICE. Stop. Now move on, please.

(MARY, CAMILLE, ANNIE and GRACE exercise in awkward silence for at least 15 seconds. The tension is thick.)

VOICE. Move on, please.

CAMILLE. *(gingerly changing the subject)* Do you ever wonder whose voice that is?

ANNIE. Probably the wife of the guy who owns this place.

CAMILLE. And what if they got a divorce. Do you think he'd get someone new to do the voice? Like James Earl Jones...*(imitating his deep voice)* "Move on please"

GRACE. I don't think Darth Vader would say please.

CAMILLE. You're right. But he'd get you to exercise. *(pause)* Maybe Kathleen Turner or Bea Arthur with their deep voices. *(does a throaty imitation)* "Move on please"

ANNIE. I think you really need someone with a more feminine voice...a sex symbol like Marilyn Monroe.

(tries to imitate her breathy voice)

"Move on please"

CAMILLE. No. It should be Arnold.

(imitating the Terminator voice)

"Move on or I'll be back" Forceful. Sexy. Effective.

VOICE. Move on please.

(They all change stations.)

MARY. I have to use the rest room. Save my space in the line-up will you?

(She exits stage left. The other women stop exercising and cluster in a group.)

GRACE. Do you think she's serious?

CAMILLE. I think she's serious.

ANNIE. Serious about what?

CAMILLE. Not collecting the marigold seeds. Ever since her mother went into that assisted living place Mary's changed. She talks about retiring and traveling to places like China or Bangladesh. She's even mentioned selling the house.

GRACE. She shouldn't make any rash decisions. Her mother has only been in the home for a couple of months. If her mom gets better and comes home she will just die if those marigolds aren't blooming.

(They exchange looks.)

So to speak…

ANNIE. Why did Mary have to put her mom in a home?

CAMILLE. She couldn't take care of her by herself. I think she had a couple of mini-strokes. It was a tough decision but I think it was for the best.

GRACE. If she finds out Mary hasn't collected the marigold seeds, she'll have a major heart attack.

CAMILLE. Y'know, Grace, it would certainly help this conversation if you'd stop using terms like "she'll just die" or "major heart attack" when you speak to Mary about her mom.

ANNIE. Today's Saturday. I could help her collect the seeds this afternoon.

CAMILLE. Ask her when she comes out of the john. Here she comes.

(Everyone rushes back to their exercise stations and acts like nothing happened.)

VOICE. Move on please.

*(**MARY** comes out of the bathroom and fits into a station to continue exercising.)*

ANNIE. Um, Mary? Do you want some help collecting those seeds?

MARY. No thanks. I've made up my mind. I am not going to collect them this year.

CAMILLE. Is there anything we can say that will change your mind?

MARY. Probably not.

CAMILLE. Grace, you talk to her.

GRACE. Mary, if you don't collect those seeds, your mom will have a…

CAMILLE. *(interrupting)* Fit.

GRACE. No. I was going to say that her mom would…

CAMILLE. *(interrupting)* Be very, very sad.

GRACE. Camille, stop putting words into my mouth. I was going to say that your mom would have a broken heart. Those seeds have been passed down from year to year. You can't break the chain. It's like one of those letters. What do they call those letters, Annie?

ANNIE. Chain letters.

GRACE. Yes. Chain letters. It would be bad luck.

CAMILLE. Grace, I don't think that Mary cares about your superstitions. She's not going to be scared into this.

GRACE. Well, you were the one who told me to talk to her.

MARY. Look, I appreciate what all of you are trying to say. For once in my life I'd like to live it up a little and plant nasturtiums instead of marigolds. I have lived at home with my mom all of my life. I've been the good daughter. It's my yard now.

ANNIE. She's right, you know.

CAMILLE. I thought you were on our side.

ANNIE. There are no sides here. Mary should have a chance to plant whatever she wants.

CAMILLE. Then I'm going to come over and collect the marigold seeds.

MARY. You will not.

CAMILLE. I will. Those seeds have to be preserved. There's more to this than collecting a bunch of seeds. Those seeds have been passed down to your mom from her mom for years. You'll regret this someday.

MARY. What would you know about regret? Your life is perfect. You have a daughter who comes all the way from Florida to eat your chili and cornbread.

CAMILLE. *(Stops exercising. Everyone else slows their exercise down a bit to listen.)* I know a lot about regret. My momma left us when we were little and my grandma brought us up. The only thing I had to remember my momma by was a picture grandma gave me. And when I was 18 we had a fire which destroyed the whole place. We lost all the family pictures…all the memories…every connection to the mother we never knew.

VOICE. Stop. Time to check your heart rate. Ready. Begin.

(The women check their heart rates.)

VOICE. Stop. Now move on please.

MARY. I'm sorry. But why shouldn't I be able to do what I want to do? All these years – collect the seeds, store the seeds, plant the seeds. And make sure you don't share the seeds! I've taken care of those marigolds my entire life.

VOICE. Move on please.

MARY. *(addressing the* **VOICE***)* YES. I'd like to…Oh "VOICE OF THE TAPE"

GRACE. I'm telling you, you'll regret it.

VOICE. Move on please.

CAMILLE. You've got to collect those seeds.

VOICE. Move on please.

CAMILLE. You've got to preserve the connections.

VOICE. Move on please.

GRACE. *(shouting to someone offstage)* The voice is going crazy again. Can you turn it off? Yeah, we'll watch the clock.

(to the exercising women)

This happened last week…just about killed me until I realized what was going on.

ANNIE. I think Mary is right.

MARY. Thank you, Annie. I really love nasturtiums.

ANNIE. No one is telling you not to plant nasturtiums. But we are telling you to pay attention to the tree stump and the big black snake.

MARY. What?

CAMILLE. Explain.

GRACE. Switch.

(They all change stations.)

ANNIE. You were afraid of the snake when you were little, right?

MARY. Terrified.

ANNIE. And your mom was there to tell you that it wouldn't hurt you, right?

MARY. Right.

ANNIE. And eventually you realized that she was right and you went back to the pond and got the seeds in spite of your fear, right?

MARY. Right.

ANNIE. And your mom also said that nothing would grow in that tree stump, correct?

MARY. Yes. But I filled it with the right soil and fertilizer and I watered it every day.

ANNIE. And how did you know which soil to add and what fertilizer to use?

MARY. My mom.

ANNIE. That's the point.

GRACE. I get it. Switch.

(They change stations.)

It's the lessons that came along with collecting the seeds, planting the seeds and harvesting the seeds over and over again that have made you who you are today. You learned about conquering your fears and how to coax life into things that didn't have a chance to grow.

ANNIE. Look, I haven't told any of you about this but when I was 12 my mom was diagnosed with breast cancer. By the time I was 13 she had passed. I have so few lessons

ANNIE. *(cont.)* from her that I remember but each day I try to live my life with the courage she had during that last year. Mary, you have a lifetime of lessons tied up in those seeds. You have to harvest the marigold seeds… AND make room for the nasturtiums.

VOICE. *(returning)* Stop. Time to check your heart rate. Ready. Begin.

(They pause to take their heart rates.)

Stop. Now move on, please.

(No one moves. They are waiting for Mary to say something.)

MARY. OK.

(They move to a new station.)

But if I make room for other kinds of flowers, I will have too many marigold seeds to plant next spring.

CAMILLE. I WANT SOME! I've been waiting to get my hands on them for years.

GRACE. Actually, so have I. They are so beautiful. And there are so many different kinds!

CAMILLE. And every time I'd ask your mother if I could have some of those seeds she'd say, "All in good time, Camille."

ANNIE. Would your mom care if we spread them all over town?

MARY. If you help me collect them, I think it would only be fair to give you some of the seeds.

CAMILLE. Won't that impress the "Beautiful America" committee next year. Everywhere they look they'd see those marigolds.

GRACE. I don't think we're planting them to impress the committee, Camille.

CAMILLE. You're right. We're spreadin' your mommas' love and care all over town…making new connections.

MARY. I don't think it would kill her if I shared those seeds…

(Everyone stops a moment to look at **MARY.** *)*

MARY. *(cont.)*…so to speak.

CAMILLE. *(pause)* What do you say, Mary?

VOICE. *(The* **VOICE** *resumes.)* Move on please.

MARY. I do feel a little wicked spreading those seeds around town after my mom hoarded them all these years. *(pause)* But she did say "All in good time"…I think this IS the "good time." *(pause)* OK.

(She stops exercising.)

I will harvest the marigold seeds from the front yard, back yard, side yard, by the fountain, around the shed and back by the big black snake. I will store them in the cracked canning jars and I will keep them separated. BUT, I will also share the seeds with you. And next year, I will plant nasturtiums *(pause)* And maybe some gladiolas...red ones...and hollyhocks...And carnations...definitely carnations...I love their smell.

CAMILLE. Whoa. Slow down. You're gonna be sore if you do that all in one day.

MARY. But I've got your help. Half hour's up... I've got to stretch now.

CAMILLE. I'll join you. Now that you've decided to share the seeds, I'm not letting you out of my sight!

MARY. Y'know, I think I'll plant some of the seeds in a pot and take them over to my mom.

(She begins to exit.)

CAMILLE. She'd love that. But let's not tell her right away about giving some of the seeds away.....

(She exits.)

GRACE. What do you say we crank it up a little, Annie. We need some extra energy if we're going to help collect those seeds this afternoon.

*(With a burst of energy, **ANNIE & GRACE** exercise to an upbeat song. They can even join in singing along. The lights fade.)*

VOICE. Move on please. Move on please. Move on.... please.

(The music gets louder. Blackout. The End.)

LIMBO

Synopsis

What happens to Limbo when the Pope decrees it will no longer exist? That's what the two caretakers of Limbo want to know. For all of eternity, Augusta and Thomasina have been taking care of all the unbaptized babies who have been denied access to heaven. Augusta pleads with Thomasina to understand that they stand on the brink of Hell while Thomasina assumes that they will be admitted into Heaven. Their argument is interrupted by the disappearance of all the babies and by God who has an urgent request.

Characters

(Three women)

AUGUSTA
THOMASINA
GOD

Offstage sounds of babies: happy baby sounds and crying baby sounds.

Set

One space and a couple of chairs. A computer is set up on a table and a small table with books, scrolls, and papers on it.

Time

Now.

Costumes

AUGUSTA - An apron and casual clothes
THOMASINA - Casual clothes
GOD - T-shirt and a sweatshirt or hoodie. The shirt could have something on it like "Almighty" or "It's not nice to fool Mother Nature"

LIMBO was a finalist in the Eileen Heckart Senior Drama Play Competition, 2007. The play had two dramatic readings at The Dark Room in Cleveland, Ohio and the Ohio State University. It was produced by Red Hen Theatre in August of 2007, directed by Rose Leininger with the cast of Michael Rubin, Elizabeth R. Wood, and Amy Pawlukiewicz.

(AT RISE: The stage is dark.)

(Lights up onstage and we see **THOMASINA** *sitting in a chair reading the newspaper. She suddenly becomes animated.)*

THOMASINA. My God! My God! *(looking up)* Thank you! *(shouting)* Augusta!

AUGUSTA. *(offstage)* I'm taking care of the babies!

THOMASINA. *(excitedly looks at the paper again)* I can't believe it! My God! Augusta, put the babies down and get out here. *(to herself)* Oh my God! Thank You. Thank You, dear God!

*(***AUGUSTA** *enters. She is wearing an apron and her hair is all disheveled. The noise of babies fades out.)*

AUGUSTA. What is so important that I have to leave the babies?

THOMASINA. *(still repeating to herself)* Thank You, God. Thank you.

(to Augusta)

Augusta, it's happened!

AUGUSTA. What? What's happened?

THOMASINA. Sit down. Sit down.

(She sits. Pause.)

We are going home.

AUGUSTA. What are you talking about? This IS our home.

THOMASINA. No. No, this was never meant to be our permanent home. Remember when we first came here? They said it would be temporary.

AUGUSTA. I don't remember that. I do remember that we came here because we weren't baptized, just like the babies. But that was some time ago.

(gets up and walks)

27

AUGUSTA. *(cont.)* I don't want to leave. I love this place. I love being with you and the babies.

THOMASINA. *(sitting her down again)* We have no choice.

AUGUSTA. Who says?

THOMASINA. They say.

AUGUSTA. Who's THEY?

THOMASINA. Here – read it yourself.

(She gives her the paper.)

AUGUSTA. *(reading)* "The Vatican established a Theological Commission today to re-examine its teachings on Limbo. Limbo has long been the subject of violent disagreements from the very beginnings of the Catholic Church. The belief in Limbo, a place where unbaptized souls go to wait for the second coming of Christ, may be eliminated from the tradition of the Catholic Church." *(slowly, sadly)* Oh, my God.

THOMASINA. *(happily)* I know. I know! No more being sandwiched between Heaven and Hell! No more long nights listening to the screeching of tormented souls on one side and yearning to be part of a choir of angels on the other.

AUGUSTA. It doesn't say that. It says we're being eliminated. You, me, the others.

THOMASINA. No. No. God would never do that.

AUGUSTA. This is not God. This is the hierarchy of the Catholic Church.

THOMASINA. Can they do that?

AUGUSTA. Remember the Inquisition? God wasn't behind that, but it happened.

THOMASINA. I just assumed.

AUGUSTA. Never assume.

THOMASINA. Well, it's just a committee. It'll be a long time before the Pope approves it.

AUGUSTA. It's just a matter of time. Why are they doing this to us?

THOMASINA. I have no idea.

AUGUSTA. The babies! What will happen to the babies?

THOMASINA. I assumed we'd bring them along into the eternal bliss of the presence of God.

AUGUSTA. But we're not baptized. They're not baptized. No baptism, no Heaven. Those are the rules.

THOMASINA. Maybe they changed the rules. Let me see that paper. I might have missed something.

(She looks through the paper.)

Nope. Nothing. Maybe AOL has something.

(She moves to the computer and sits and types. **AUGUSTA** *follows looking over her shoulder.)*

Here. AOL has a survey. "Where would the souls in Limbo go?" 67% undecided. I hope God doesn't have the internet.

AUGUSTA. Are you kidding? God invented it.

THOMASINA. I thought it was Al Gore…

AUGUSTA. No. GOD.

THOMASINA. There's another question in the survey but I'm not sure you want to know the answer.

AUGUSTA. Faced with the end of my existence, could things get any worse?

THOMASINA. Should Limbo exist? 95% said no.

(Pause. She walks back to the chair and sits.)

What are we going to do? I want to see the Face of God again. From what I remember, God was awesome.

AUGUSTA. Maybe if we just stay put. Wait. I remember reading something.

(She gets up and searches for something. She finds a scroll and blows the dust off of it, unrolls it and begins to read.)

Here it is…."Limbo will be replaced by bliss when the messianic kingdom is established"

THOMASINA. How old is that document?

AUGUSTA. 1140 AD

THOMASINA. *(She types something into the computer.)* Wikipedia says, "the *souls* of those dying in mortal *sin* or in *original sin* go down at once into *Hell*, to be punished, however, with widely different penalties." What is that? Widely different penalties?

AUGUSTA. Mortal sinners burn. Limbo residents toast lightly?

THOMASINA. I don't want to toast. I want to see the Face of God. I've put my time in. Taking care of all the unbaptized babies in the universe is no picnic. Feeding them alone has taken eons…and changing their diapers…

AUGUSTA. You never did that.

THOMASINA. Sometimes – sometimes I did.

AUGUSTA. Maybe…twice.

THOMASINA. OK. Twice. *(pause)* God has forgotten about us. I mean, here we are in Limbo, living on the fringes of heaven and hell…being good…taking care of all the babies….making sure that they don't accidentally fall into the fiery pit of Hell…feeding them…singing them to sleep…We just need to remind God about everything we've done since we got here.

AUGUSTA. Aren't you forgetting something?

THOMASINA. What?

AUGUSTA. *(She finds a book.)* Here. The Baltimore Catechism. Lesson number 2

THOMASINA. How old is that?

AUGUSTA. *(proudly)* 1942. Practically written yesterday.

"When we say God is all-knowing we mean that God knows all things, past, present and future even our most secret thoughts, words and actions."

God knows we're here. God has not forgotten us.

THOMASINA. I don't think so. Whoa – our most secret thoughts, words and actions? I think I may be in trouble.

AUGUSTA. Thomasina, God doesn't care if you don't change the babies' diapers.

THOMASINA. I'm not talking about that.

AUGUSTA. What are you talking about?

THOMASINA. Well, sometimes – I think about – y'know…

AUGUSTA. What?

THOMASINA. Well…about the beatific vision. I only saw God once so I try to remember what GOD looks like.

AUGUSTA. That's not a bad thing. It's probably flattering- I mean, how many people down there actually think about God? They have more important things to think about like *who's* going to conquer *who* to get *what* land. Let them try living on the hem of eternity taking care of all the unbaptized babies in the universe.

THOMASINA. Yeah. You're right. But I don't want to be eliminated and I don't want to go to Hell. We have to work on a plan to get to heaven before the hierarchy gets rid of Limbo.

AUGUSTA. *(reading from the scroll)* "Unbaptized children will not only enjoy perfect, natural *happiness*, but they will *rise with immortal bodies* on the *last day* and have the renovated earth for their *happy* abode" Hey, we just have to sit tight and be patient.

THOMASINA. Until the very last day? It could be awhile. And that was written in the 1100's. Things have changed.

AUGUSTA. Things haven't changed that much.

THOMASINA. On the subject of Limbo, things have changed a lot. Here.

(She crosses to the computer.)

I'll GOOGLE…

(spelling out loud)

L I M B O.

AUGUSTA. You can Google or swim the net all you like….

THOMASINA. *(gently interrupting her)* Surf the net. You surf the net.

AUGUSTA. Surf all you want but I am staying here until God tells me otherwise.

(She notices something on the computer screen.)

What is that?

THOMASINA. Clips from a TV show. Auditions for USA Starstruck

AUGUSTA. What?

THOMASINA. USA Starstruck. It's a program where people try to be America's next singing star. It's the number one TV show.

AUGUSTA. Really?

THOMASINA. It's very popular...Wait a minute. Wait a minute. Thinking...thinking...I've got an idea...

AUGUSTA. I'm going to check the babies.

THOMASINA. No, wait. I think we could do the same thing. Listen. On earth they have these auditions to win big prizes. They win money...

AUGUSTA. The root of all evil.

THOMASINA. They win other things. Some people even tryout to sing with celebrities at the Grammy Awards.

AUGUSTA. The Granny awards?

THOMASINA. No, no. The Grammy Awards. Look, the church is going to erase Limbo like a smudge from its history. We need to let someone know we exist and that we are worthy of Heaven before they send us to Hell. In order to prove that we deserve Heaven, we need to audition...to try out.

AUGUSTA. *(pause)* How do we try out for Heaven?

THOMASINA. I have no idea. But we have the internet and television to help us figure it out. Are you with me?

AUGUSTA. No matter what happens, we're taking the babies with us, right?

THOMASINA. Of course. They're the reason we're doing all this. Those babies don't belong in Hell getting lightly toasted. And they can't audition. They'll just drool on the judges. We can audition for them. If we get in, then we take them with us.

AUGUSTA. OK. What do you want me to do?

THOMASINA. There's a lot of singing in Heaven. The Chorus of Angels is huge, so God must like singing. Maybe if we prove we can sing it will show God that we belong in Heaven.

AUGUSTA. You're right! I've never heard any singing in Hell, just a lot of this

(She screeches.)

and that

(She squawks.)

THOMASINA. That sounds a lot like the last winner of USA Starstruck. *(short pause)* That's it! We should rehearse an audition like they have on that TV show. I know all about it. I'll pretend to be the person trying out and you pretend to be the judge.

AUGUSTA. I don't know how to be a judge. Why can't I be the person trying out? I've had some experience doing community theatre.

THOMASINA. OK. You need a song. You got a song?

AUGUSTA. Yes!

THOMASINA. You walk out of the room...

AUGUSTA. I sing in the hall?

THOMASINA. No. You walk out of the room so you can turn around and walk into the room.

AUGUSTA. Why can't I stay right here and sing?

THOMASINA. Look, you want to get into Heaven, right? Then we have to do what USA Starstruck does... exactly.

AUGUSTA. OK. How do you know all this?

THOMASINA. The internet. They have an online feed.

AUGUSTA. So while I am feeding the babies you are online feeding?

THOMASINA. More or less. Go out of the room and when you come in you have to act really scared or really rude.

AUGUSTA. Do I have another choice?

THOMASINA. Nope.

AUGUSTA. Are you sure?

THOMASINA. Positive. In fact we should probably practice it both ways.

AUGUSTA. OK.

(She leaves the room. **THOMASINA** *arranges the furniture so that she is sitting at a small table in a chair.* **AUGUSTA** *enters again, very shy and retiring.)*

AUGUSTA. Hi. I'd like to sing a *little* song…

THOMASINA. *(perhaps with an English accent)* As little as possible, please. Get on with it!

AUGUSTA. Thomasina, you don't have to be so mean!

THOMASINA. *(drops the accent)* Augusta, that's the way they act. Please, trust me.

AUGUSTA. OK.

(Quietly she sings just first words of "You are My Sunshine.")

"You are my sunshine, my only sunsh.....

THOMASINA. *(yelling)* STOP. Stop singing…and I use the term lightly. You stink. No, you smell worse than last week's trash. Leave this room right now before I puke.

AUGUSTA. *(She can't believe her ears.)* OK.

THOMASINA. Great Augusta! Now go out again and this time, try to be rude to me.

AUGUSTA. All right.

(When she re-enters she comes storming in, grabs **THOMASINA** *by the shirt and says)*

I'm going to sing this song whether you like it or not. So pipe down and listen.

(She lets go of **THOMASINA** *and she starts to sing the same song loudly.)*

"You are my sunshine…

THOMASINA. *(yelling)* Are all the people in Limbo so incredibly UNtalented….and ugly…and absolutely, undeniably putrid. Who told you that you could sing? Get out! Go on, GET OUT!!!

AUGUSTA. *(genuinely hurt)* I'm sorry. I was just trying to do the best I could for the babies.

(She begins to cry and starts to leave, sincerely shook up.)

THOMASINA. That was perfect!

AUGUSTA. What?

THOMASINA. Those babies will be walking through the pearly gates tonight.

AUGUSTA. You yelled at me! You made me cry!

THOMASINA. YES!

(She hugs her.)

And you were the perfect blend of arrogance and heartbreak. Where did you learn to act like that?

AUGUSTA. Well, I played a hollyhock in a show sponsored by the Linden Ladies Breakfast Club and I...Wait, what makes you think that God is going to let us into heaven acting this way.

THOMASINA. Look, this stuff works for those people on earth. It should work for us.

AUGUSTA. Not for me. I'd rather wait until the end of time. I quit. This is a mean-spirited, nasty bit of reality. Even God wouldn't like it. God is love.

THOMASINA. But your audition was better than anything online...Here, look.

(She works on the computer. AUGUSTA watches the screen and reacts in horror, She with interest as they watch a clip online.)

See? That guy right there went on to make a CD that made a lot of money.

And you're way better than him.

(looks at the computer screen and clicks on something)

Oh, no.

AUGUSTA. What?

THOMASINA. It's an AOL bulletin. It says that the commission recommended to the Pope that he abolish Limbo today. *(pause)* Today, Augusta. *(pause)* Please, Augusta, we have to keep rehearsing. If not for us, then for the babies.

THOMASINA. We need work together. Audition together. Sing a song together.

AUGUSTA. A duet?

THOMASINA. A love song.

AUGUSTA. God IS love.

THOMASINA. Do you know any love songs?

AUGUSTA. I haven't sung anything except lullabies in a long time.

THOMASINA. Well, a lullaby is a kind of love song. It's now or never.

AUGUSTA. *(She begins to sing "All Through the Night," An Irish folk song.)*

Sleep my child and peace attend thee,

All through the night

Guardian angels God will send thee,

All through the night

(THOMASINA joins her in singing.)

Soft the drowsy hours are creeping,

Hill and dale in slumber sleeping

I my loved ones' watch am keeping

All through the night.

THOMASINA. That was beautiful. I think the babies are all asleep.

AUGUSTA. Well, I couldn't have done it without you. Singing to all of the unbaptized babies in the universe is a two person job.

THOMASINA. Y'know, maybe that's the song we should use for the audition.

AUGUSTA. If it doesn't put God to sleep. I'll check on the babies.

(She exits. She screams offstage and then rushes back onstage.)

AUGUSTA. *(cont.)* They're gone!

THOMASINA. What?

AUGUSTA. The babies are gone.

(THOMASINA rushes off stage to check. She returns immediately.)

THOMASINA. I'll look outside. If they've crawled near that fiery pit...

(**GOD** *enters. She is dressed in a sweatshirt and jeans or something casual.*)

GOD. They're all gone. All the souls in Limbo.

THOMASINA. Who are you?

GOD. I know it's been a long time but I didn't think you'd forget me.

AUGUSTA. How did you know that the babies were gone?

GOD. Baltimore Catechism. Lesson number two. God knows all things, past present and....

AUGUSTA. Are you???

GOD. Yes. I am. Always was...always will be and always remains the same.

AUGUSTA. Dressed like that?

GOD. It's Sunday. My day off. Even God gets a break from all that heavenly bliss. I like to walk around incognito and see what's really going on...keep up with the news...

THOMASINA. Then you know about Limbo?

GOD. Bitter, bitter argument...been around for thousands of years. Today, it's resolved. Limbo is no more.

THOMASINA. Limbo's gone? Where did the babies go?

AUGUSTA. Yes, where are the babies?

GOD. They're all safe where they belong. Your "audition" worked. Your lullabye sent everyone straight to Heaven when the Pope dissolved Limbo today. Great idea... singing a song of love.

THOMASINA. See, I told you God would like it!

AUGUSTA. But we're HERE. If everyone else is in Heaven, we must be headed for the other place.

GOD. Well, there's a little matter of getting a job.

THOMASINA. We had a job. It's time for heavenly retirement.

GOD. Well, these days everyone in Heaven has a job.
How long have you two been watching those babies?

THOMASINA. In terms of years or diapers changed?

AUGUSTA. You never changed their diapers.

THOMASINA. Twice.

AUGUSTA. Oh my God…

GOD. Yes, I am.

AUGUSTA. I see where You're going with this. You want us to take care of the babies in Heaven.

GOD. They aren't babies anymore. Once they entered Heaven they transformed into, well, *(pause)* teenagers. They don't need you like they did before. But I need you. I have a job for both of you if you are willing to take it.

THOMASINA. Why do you need a job in Heaven?

GOD. Since all the baby boomers started passing over into this life we need to keep everyone busy. It's unbelievably crowded! And now we have all these young souls to keep in line until they learn about heaven and how things are done here. We have our hands full.

AUGUSTA. And what would you have us do, Lord?

GOD. We've never had so many teenagers here before and frankly, you two are the only ones that have some kind of emotional connection with them.
We need to teach them about living in Heaven. They'll listen to you. Will you help us out the next couple of years? I promise when they learn what they need to know, I'll let you two retire to a beautiful little spot of eternal bliss.

AUGUSTA. Well, I would like to see them again…

THOMASINA. Augusta, are you crazy? Do you think that this is going to be in any way, shape or form, similar to taking care of those cute little babies? All we had to do was keep those babies fed and dry and away from the burning pit of Hell. Teenagers invented the burning pit of Hell!

(short pause)

AUGUSTA. Thomasina, God needs us. We've been through an eternal infancy with these kids. We need to help them through these next years.

THOMASINA. *(pause as she thinks)* How many years until we can retire?

GOD. A hundred years, tops.

AUGUSTA. What do you say, Thomasina?

THOMASINA. All right. But retirement is looking mighty good to me and we haven't even started.

AUGUSTA. I think I'll go on ahead. I wonder if they'll remember me?

GOD. They're all waiting to see you just inside the gates.

AUGUSTA. Thanks. Will there ever be a chance to take care of babies again?

GOD. Babies go right to Heaven now. It's the law.

AUGUSTA. Thomasina was right. You are awesome.

(She exits.)

THOMASINA. I've been thinking about this and I think there should be parental controls on the internet.

GOD. Great idea.

*(**GOD** and **THOMASINA** start to exit.)*

THOMASINA. I'm glad we're on the same page here. *(thinking)* And they have to have a curfew.

GOD. Absolutely.

THOMASINA. God, You are awesome!

GOD. That's what they say.

THOMASINA. And no one, I mean *no one*, is allowed to go near the brink of Hell.

GOD. That goes without saying.

THOMASINA. How old do they have to be to drive up here? Or do they get wings??? I'm gonna need wings just to keep up with them….

*(**GOD** and **THOMASINA** exit.)*

(blackout)

The End

Also by
Maureen Brady Johnson...

Shoes Along the Highway

Please visit our website **samuelfrench.com** for complete
descriptions and licensing information